LIFE AND DEATH IN THE STONE AGE

Eric Zeidler was born of Russian Jewish parents in January 1962 in Warsaw, but grew up in Dallas, Texas, where he was educated at the prestigious Highland Park School (1974-81). He spent most of the next three and a half years in Northern California, at Stanford University in Palo Alto. By 1985 Zeidler had moved to New York City to try and publish his first novel. Publication proved elusive, and beset with feelings of depression and alienation, he began using Narcotics. In 1988, he moved back to Dallas and a year later went into a treatment programme for drug dependency. In 1998 he moved back to New York with his then-girlfriend, but was forced to return to Dallas in 2001, after the girlfriend suffered a complete psychotic breakdown. Fired from his job at a local bookstore, he unexpectedly secured employment at the Dallas Museum of Art, where he was befriended by a number of kindred spirits. His friendship with Jeff Zilm, an Artist, led him to re-examine the efficacy and potential of poetry within the discouraging context of modern American life. Re-inspired by the encouragement he received from Zilm, he embarked on a new cycle of poems, loosely tying in with the cornerstone poem, "Life and Death in the Stone Age." Zeidler currently resides in Dallas, and is said to be contemplating a collection of prose poetry and avant-garde fragments. He lives with his girlfriend, Allison Low, and his three cats, Dixie Martinovna, Snegurichka, and Dzhonoushka.

By Eric Tomasovich Zeidler

The Collected Diaries: 1979 – 1983
(edited by Jane Soslowski)

The Truths That Won't Stop

Paparazzi Summer

In preparation:

Red Cell Ghosts: Collected Stories and Fragments

Strange Holiday

Shingle Springs (A Story of First Love)

ERIC ZEIDLER

LIFE AND DEATH IN THE STONE AGE

Selected and edited by
Simon Miklovicz and Jonathan Angel-Sadis

TSEKH POETOV
An Imprint of Mad Tom *Publishers*

First published in the USA 2009 by
Tsekh Poetov
an imprint of Mad Tom Publishers
30 Miller Avenue
Dallas, Texas 75206
audumlasvyataya@aol.com

Cover photograph by Timothy C. Merritt

Printed and bound in USA by
Lulu.com
ISBN 978-0-578-02456-1 pbk.

CONTENTS

ACKNOWLEDGMENTS

The author would like to acknowledge and thank his family, Ann Ralston, Susannah Benedetti, and Carol Anne Burtchaell; his common-law spouse, Allison Low; his comrades, Evelyn Zeidler, Jeff Zilm, and Christopher Andrews; his psychologist, Dr. Barry S. Coakley; his three cats, Dixie Martinovna, Marigold Snegurichka, and Little Dzhonouskha; and his friends, Mary Ferrell, Bruce Curll, Charlotte McDougal, Kristen Painter, J.C. Bigornia, Tomas Geczy, Roan Conrad, Barbara Ann Davis, Trafton Bogert, Janis Perkins, Karyn Feiden, David Elsasser, Paula McFarland, Beatrix and Garth Sampson, Cathy Zisk, Tamara Wootton-Bonner, Tennessee Bonner, Coleman Bonner, Kevin Parmer, Andrew Culler, Ron Moody, and Andre Anthony for their unwavering encouragement and support.

A NOTE ON THE TEXT

These poems are arranged in a rough chronological order. Zeidler began writing poetry in 1978, but most of the Juvenilia, in his opinion and those of the editors, are overly derivative, and do not merit inclusion in this collection. Zeidler went through several periods of complete silence (as regards poetry), and this helps explain the chronological gaps the reader will encounter. Finally, a number of poems were written, discarded, and then reconstituted years later. The criterion for dating these 'hybrids' proved fairly subjective. In the editors' judgement, if enough of the original remained, it was placed in its original time sequence. If alterations predominated, the work was moved forward. Zeidler did not date or sequence his poems, and a certain amount of guesswork has necessarily been involved.

"The Namesake"

Whoever said that anything is known
Is fortunate, for, stupid, he will rise
As sages fall; extremity alone
Provides the standard; even as we shift,
Dissolving vortices or painting sweeps
Which swerve obliquely, dizzily unknown
To former state—now, even as the flakes
Accelerate and clump, yes, even now—
We know not whether poles effectuate
The fluxion, or, belike unto a plough,
Are often seen as by the furrows moved,
And not the other way; perhaps the rows
Do yawn of their volition to propel
The implement. Each pew of Holy Church
Lifts up shared supplication to the Rose,
The Star, the Hammer, and the Winged Lion.
They constitute all else, and who are *they*?
The symbols, or the otherwise inane
Caressing sprigs of fashionable thought?
Each warbling tributary, every ray
Of sunlight, juxtaposèd, illustrates
The garden's dual love, its dual slough

Of crumbly, heat-cracked, worm-infested clods.

We nothing know, save something, as it nods—

For slothful slovenliness cannot itself

Debase for long in cuckolding its namesake.

Yea, do not worry; worry yet too much—

A balance in the middle forms a pole,

Imbalance made the mean, and it a pole—

Live thus, forsooth, encircling the goal

That from thyself must win its purest weal,

And one not stolen, neither overused.

With others let it never be confused.

1981
Dallas

And who are you to tell us how to live?
I shall not even try to learn the Truth,
For truth is nothing, anything Alone
Eludes true Possibility; I give
For giving's sake—is nothing anymore
Sufficient? Why the failure to condone?
   The two outshine the one; I counsel Life.
Three Philistines foment internal war
Where two exchange their being, always two,
Yet seeming One—strange harmony in strife!
   My words be mystic. Turn away from Truth,
And in the Turning let the mind construe
Whatever thoughts it will, so long as each
But springs from what a year ago in youth
You turn'd away from, coming face to face
With new-formed words that deviously reach
Old ways abandoned, making of the world
A larger thing, or smaller, full of Grace
According to Itself, for many make
But two again, a double flag unfurl'd
By single wind, and all as you had guessed!
   We know as in a dream, and we awake
Too seldom when without the force of will,
The beauty, ah the Love, the blatantest
Of all, but of the other must I speak;

The covert Half, and typically, until
You chase it with a vengeance, you will ache,
Bereft of both, when both, as both are weak,
Should help each other trudge along the path;
Each step accomplished serves further to wake
Our destiny, the path too long for sight
To penetrate, though in the aftermath
We shall, I think, discover that we trod
A circle vast whereof each equal site
Is farthest from one other of them all,
One other alone, and *this*, I think, is God.

II.

The trickling waters cannot supersede
Pale wafers that they buoy up in their midst.
No duck nor greedy heron here can feed;
It is the incarnation of a creed
That for each different being yields a Soul
More different yet, except that all do bleed.
And for those wafers light enough to float
One wonders if there ever were a goal
In making, thus, their plight so difficult;
In making Beauty rather than a boat.

The Host is far away; I feel my heart
Beat slower at the distance's assault,
As rippling waves oppugn the placid flow
Originally meant to play apart
From all the turmoil endlessly sustained,
And for a reason has it all been so,
Albeit not a one foreseen by them
Who valued Grace enough to see it veined
With life-sustaining agony, that both
At any cost might harden from the phlegm
Of what alone is victory for Ill.
  Who first descried from eyries of her growth
The message? Who was rare enough to try
The balmy flight that from a certain chill
To languid warmth may peradventure lead?
The property of motion, like the sky,
Is but an arm of Being, whether cloud
Or thick stagnation bring about the deed
Of slaughter which reacts, but never *does*.
  If wafers crumble, being neither proud
Nor avaricious, how shall we survive?
Some know not that there ever even was
A better life, a state more nigh the birth
When, strangers to despair, we strangely
     thrive,

Not dreaming that in time we shall ingest,

Unknowingly, a manufactured worth—

And of which all the minted, golden coins

Are but the excrement of souls oppressed

Yet clothed in worldly metal; I suspect

That suffering springs also from the loins

Of first creation—beings in their sheen

Extend ensuing Loss from the effect

Of being *made*, of, then, surrendering

A trifle more than later might have been.

  It doesn't matter; rivers will suffice

In all their sullied splendors, in the sting

of Beauty—endless beauty, endless pangs—

Sublimity extreme yet imprecise!

  And yet, all streams not stagnant ply a course

Replete with underwater barbs and fangs.

Because in its consistence water draws

A blood invisible, it is the source

Of suffering that is too highly keyed,

It never helps itself, and just because

You do not see the blood, it suffers more—

The stream that taught Existence how to bleed.

  We form our own reward, unless in time

The agony destroy us; 'tis a door

With double hinges, cunningly astride

Twixt symmetry too severe and utter
   Rime-lessness.
  I counsel life. Survive, and see the path
Diminish in a width that grows more wide
When walked upon; survive by what is best
For *You*. Do not explain. Ignore blind Wrath,
Observing how the stream will die; how two
Will help each other, whilst a single quest
Conjoins them as a unit to the Will
They serve, that both may doubly Love and Do.

August 1981
Dallas

Iniquity all stacked beneath the stars
In semblance of a mighty red-bricked tower
Surmounted by an emerald turning round
And round again, revolving drunkenly
Atop the layered paradoxes, must
Beyond a point collapse, the surprise, regret,
And incredulity surpassing thought,
Dissecting bricks intelligible—there
The genius lies—place side by side the two—
Yea, build upon them, layers jutting out
From neighbourly ill-mixture, and behold
An edifice that emanates the spokes
One at a time, contrasting light with dark,
Reversing back, or halting altogether,
Then starting up again from greater height,
The mortar'd loaves ne'er knowing when its beam
Will replicate them further, stretch the seam
More tight—but not enough for what they want.
  They got it, though, with interest on the day
That he unbreakable unjoined himself
To drain a fermenting cask of stolen mare's milch.
Beloved, you and I are far away
From everything we vainly think most near.
Stay with me as I spin the chosen tale.
Leave not without remembering that what

Befell our folk may cancel your return.

In staying with me, after all, you join

Your soul to mine; there's nowhere else a link,

Not in the things you murder, hoard, or think.

We do all three, and three times two is six;

While three times six will bring it back unless

The one is added, one who knows the use

Of masonry, and mixing elements

Quite different, as with clockwork algebra,

Or, better yet, the birthplace of its sway.

  Vadim was such an one; his triple code

Of beauty, truth, and love inspired the young,

Unlocked their thinking, filled them with burning zeal.

Artur and Katya, Zyr, and Sherifer,

The Gentle Thorn, she also trod the maze

From contact maddening—they all put forth

Their scimitars of ivory, their wails

That never shall the desert wind forget.

  The Sacred City, clouded since a time

Of fairer things, enclosed within its walls

Vadim who ran the gamut of emotion

In shaping thought to fortify his art.

An artist, he was one of that strange tribe

Who puts art through the wringer, save that Art

Will never suffer earth to slip away.

Like drops of honey oozing through a sluice
His only rival, sowing sparks of bliss,
Was Vlad, whose very cradle turned to ash
From contact with the firebrand never meant
Likewise to burn, all armoured thus in flame.
  The Tower's lowest tiers were laid when they,
So great, so like, so close, did fail to meet,
For high enough in structure was Vadim
To be aloof from segments which by nature
Contained the Other, one who hated what
Had spared him from the pallid welts it raised
On delicate Vadim's deceiving strength.
At times this noble artist caught a breath
Of things so dreadful that he well nigh swoon'd.
Obsessed he was with luck's cold-bloodedness,
A morbid hour here and there consum'd
In wondering how fast he should have died
If born a peasant, as the odds would favour
For souls unborn and thusly under no
Implicit obligation, for he felt
Ungrateful in a moodiness of soul
Unlikely to diminish on demand.
Then also, as the darling of a set
Well placed, yet vigilant, he sensed their eyes
Ever on him, fitfully expecting yields

Luxurious and promising from one

In whom so many harvestings were sown.

Concealment of a nature petulant,

Disposed to sloth and inconsistent lusts,

And with these flaws the sensitive caress

Of pupils bottomless became a fixed

And daily flail of anguish barbed with yearning.

He yearned for devotion less like a gaoler's cell

Than couch so supple that the butterfly

Might rest its wings of radiance thereon,

And in his mania to feel the touch

Of wings impalpable and velvet poised

To, by example, fly away itself,

Vadim disliked most heartily the sites

That in their tragedy had once been sacred.

  On other days he met, in ones or twos,

The faction that defiled whatever it

Might come to know, for by its postulates

The sundry group defin'd

The course of his concealment, liable

To change with company, inside the bound

Of what they somehow always, in their hordes,

Arrived at—what Vadim had never known:

Consensus, with the others, or alone.

  As with his anguish, particles of pride

Engendered scorn toward these practices,

So that he could not understand the trend

That lately was restructuring his life.

In former times, not breaking bread with others,

He revel'd in scouring the ancient scrolls

That filled the shelves to overflowing, stacked

Throughout the halls of mild Selim, his sire.

The words, back then, impatient seemed to fuse

With one another, fettering the soul

In toils of sturgeon slices, in caviar

Made self-regenerative beside the sea.

An elastic-lipped omniscience would take him back

To zones far different from the empty here and now,

To glimpses of the Prophet, whose burning eyes,

So rounded, did suggest the sun and moon,

Whose voice came from afar and pierced the deafness

Of closed-off hubris, wine-besotted pride,

Whose sonorous tragedy, indeed, whose death

Back then used up a surfeit of compassion.

Such was the toll of seething conflagrations

Within him that of late he rather saw

The sentence, not the word, and it dissolved

Instead of fusing, made at last a line

Of alphabetic characters, a field

Of buried corpses which he then exhumed

Painstakingly to reconnect the sense.

    And so it was that, of his verses tired,
Vadim accompanied a caravan
Beyond Mount Ararat, then told his folk
By messenger that he was deathly ill,
And thereby won permission for to bide.
The act of deviously going on
To take the emerald waters of the sea
Was like unbuttoning his outer skin,
Emerging from the body that his circle
Still monitored, and flying on the wind.
The Caspian should never be described;
Too holy is its pristine needlework,
A sloping cheek of green obsidian,
A haunch of jade that emanates the mist
Of luminous embroidery; it called
To Vadim as the rough entraps the smooth,
The mute the muted, twine the highly strung,
For where the catfish leaps, there leaps unseen
A leaping that with ease from sheen to sheen
Trails languid fingers neither small nor large,
But growing dank or buoyant with the barge.
    He gathered pebbles, waded in the surf,
And wanted but for complementary
Companionship, a solace for the gaps

He trenchantly perceived within himself:
A hollowness within the blinding brick
That he had moulded, sparkling with the stars
That facets sheer reflected—he did want
Most desperately to be a thing adored,
And whether this conceit insulted Love,
Or flattered it, the Prophet, alone, can say,
Pursed lips intense to bursting in their shame.
Belike an engine of intricate design,
His fragile soul of blooming tiger-lilies
Converted wretched hankerings for Love
To fields of wheat where pulsed a shimmering
And golden sinew deep inside, for he
Was, after all, alone beside the sea,
Alone, and safe, or dangerously amidst
The sources of a love and of a pain
That hurled him as a javelin high above,
That in the falling he split himself and die,
Or, point the other way, toward the earth
Drive home his will the noble way—the way
He'd seen the tranquil sun accomplish it:
With penetrating, sharpened, squint-eyed rays
Of burnished, golden, bubbling distillation.
  Beloved, when you see a spirit skirt
The outer darkness, courting detriment,

A tension in the air, the whirlwind close,

You see a reconciliation strange

Between enlightened fear, and poetry.

For him the desert's tempests held no fear,

Nor any of the savage carnivores

With whom he sympathised, for long ago

The thought of dying violently strained

His quivering neck, electrified the beams

Of Love primeval springing from his eyes—

Where now he treated corporeal death

As salt pernicious, biting, and extreme

For platters heaped with teeming, swarming locusts

Of perfect fever, life's libation sweet.

  The nightfall brought a diadem of stars

To crown the sky that crowned the very air

That formed his crown, and as Vadim reclined

Upon a gently sloping eminence

Alive with aromatic vines and flowers

He languidly enveloped and adjusted

The fur-lined cloak about his aching limbs.

The morning's walk along with wading all

The afternoon beneath the beating sun

Brought sleep to him that reverenced its sway.

October 1981
Stanford

16

Unrippling smoothness gleams complicatedly
without a break along the spine of surfaces;

who are you then to disbrace and primly stanch
the velvet slumber's wrinkled, threadbare bleeding?

To pluck at voluptuous, soft-spun tapestry
requires a palsied reaching sheathed in sighs
stretched paper-thin, diaphanous, shuddering.

All feeling creases, and in total all
the black-lipped void is nothing,
absolutely Nothing.

Fall 1981
Stanford

"Svyatapolk"

Song beautiful, so beautiful and rich,
beat sinfully sweeps out pellucid pitch
of slow continuum, so low and dark—
soft doublet for beloved, distant spark
of something else, o tell me, let me say
o please, by far too cruel that to-day
will never know to-morrow, or that I
can never reach you, be exchanges true
or false, for want of discourse renders *or*
and, and our ores of Slavic spices bleach
each tongue or tincture readiest for speech
to crocodile for salivary gland's
grey lotus symbol-mud and purple ands
in place of ors magnificent, they tell,
for years go by in time first to dispel
then under pressure glibly undeceive
repugnant fantasy whilst yellow heave
its sighs, and whisper green, and they its fits
of they-me-I against his-their-your-its,
or, worse, their *it's*—Nay go, I say, stay home,
most windy out, stay home; you turned to foam
blue lake of love, bruised blue from supple green,
and just because in time will seventeen
years, by you, have them, nay excuse to die.
Enough corrupts our furnaces, our sty—
Laugh, all our private chambers, join, abide,
and join, but first, I tell you, come inside.

January 1982
Stanford

"Paper Thin"

Her eyes will be an emptiness opaque,
Her lips a mirror for Medusan words,
Her kisses death, her breath stale, and the laugh—
Tiara crowning everything most dark.

And so It is; small wonder then the ache
Each time her image somnolently girds
My loins in armour taken from the Calf
Of Want, of all illuminings the spark.

I've seen the glitters coming, when they spake
Their ultraviolet aphorisms, herds
So sluggish that the crashing of a staff
Will scarcely strike, but whistle in the arc

By which it falls, and yet it's no mistake
That she is so, for she's behind the birds
Whose piercing cries obscure the inner half,
The vibrant soul 'neath symbol sweetly stark.

All life's a masque unshaven for the gleaner.
The pathos, all sliced up, cuts all the keener,
The gasping nobler, pain worse, venom greener
At being able to say, 'Oh yes, I've *seen* her."

January 1982
Stanford

"Concentration"

Remember what you did and how the bliss
Commingled with your black paralysis.

The paradise primeval keeps a train
Of various leaves, diurnal rose and thorn,
Soft petals, tremulous beneath the rain—
All different, rich, symbolic, yet forlorn,

A different thing in every painted eye,
In pupil delicate or wanton lash—
Pearls priceless all, all murdering, to die,
Yet live forever, fleeing vengeful smash.

Come drink, you're thirsty?

Ah, the guard prevents you.

Don't cringe to see the Commune set against you.
Hate pain, love life, relate the two and strive.
Go down on record trying to survive.

January 1982
Stanford

"La Primavera"

Dead hush
confuses living hedges as the bold
and measured tramp of feet from every side

continues, and the rouge-adorned hours
wave blankly from their passing carts which crush

initiate grains of sand into a mould
of singleness; they dance beneath the stride.

Eyes flash and flicker through and through the guile;
they see the lips, but cannot see the smile.

February? 1982
Stanford

"Flood"

Into my veins the water-hornets creep,
And yet the black umbrella seems extreme,

Its gripe a thing of crushing heaviness,
Its opening a closing off of sight.

Rain glistens on the elephant,
But where it falls, it drowns the worm.

Beware those eyes so hard the watery flow
Gives way before their searching, livid sweep.

February 1982
Stanford

22

"Colchis"

His veins could scarce contain the pulsing surge
of blood that, near to bursting, crazed the brain

with a shock restructuring the olden cast
of thoughts and feelings, formerly detached,

uplifted now, and in his laughing bloom,
the tresses woven with flowers, beauty fast

to plodding purpose, now he sings a dirge
for colours undefiled but far away.

His spirit soars and glides before the blast
of eyes exploding, someday, will emerge

to bring it down, in wandering astray.

February 1982
Stanford

"Fire Festival"

A glistening fire-flower snuffed itself
With gushing streams of blood that sprang from tongues
Of molten flame on which it rained its dross.

The shell is cracked; a quietude now settles
On deeper tragedies and knots of loss.

Will forest's tangled verdure scorch the land?
Or beauty under cultivation sire

Its own survival? Whether quivering petals
Exult or no, their precious trenches cross.

There's something close, dew-laden, venting steam.
To keep it you will hasten very, very
Serenely toward the necessary pang.

March 1982
Stanford

"Compulsive"

I dreamed a dream, or maybe had a vision
where all was dark; the driving rain was wet

as if to perforate our dry collision—
from heaven there screamed a burning whirlwind; spring

was gone forever; sin had set the claw
on children made to pay ancestral debt.

The vision came and for a week
I shivered, gasped and sniveled on the peak

of a formless mountain craggy, cold, and bare.
Oh g-d, why take all else except I speak?

March 1982
Stanford

"Striking the Match"

A child painted the remorseless hand
in giddy steams of red.

The spirit weeps, but doesn't always know
how stars expand,
sear—

sear the eyes to vapour
which swirls, as eyes, to penetrate the dead,
floats thick and sluggish, hopelessly to shower

itself with flakes of ash, and now the flower
is blooming, bleeding, dying
in its power.

March 1982
Stanford

"In the Heart of the Greenwood"

As trembling, outstretched hands lift up
and fall in waxing adoration,

the moon comes out, reflecting off of
saints and fools, sweet idiots and sullen whores,

the pushers getting unmoved movers
stoned on Hegel and Kierkegaard—

October 1982
East Palo Alto

Crisp bolts are spun on looms of woe.

No joke, I say, that snippets snip
themselves, though (face devour'd by dog,
with master's cupboard out of food)
it doesn't really hurt.

Alas, the scissors Hiroshima
  snipped as well,
    Who cares?
      Drop out.

October 1982
East Palo Alto

It's not to revel in grotesquery
that all the contemplation fazes fools,
but merely to accept.

In Holy Church
the pews yawn wide as from the pulpit
a cracked voice thunders:

"Confess, I say, reveal the hidden thing!"

And to say, "Yes, I confess, my scabrous birth
was worse than anything that since has been,"
is not so very painful, is it? Pain
retains its relativity until

the soul becomes progressive; size it up
and turn to exploitation, tobacco fields
of ever opening, ever widened, door.

The rules must reach the fore
and play commence
twixt deadly counterforces.

In the lore
of everything we flee and denigrate,
cognitive discourse bit the dust,

and this is war.

October 1982
East Palo Alto

29

"Dark Music"

Soft webs of interconnectedness
escape in waves, brocaded now,
now rent in tearing sympathy
toward what the bird of night threads forth,
and all throughout the moonlit grass,
the slender trees and fountain, still
with midnight, thick paralysis—
they feel it all in equal measure,
but most of all the snails, for snails
best choreograph the dance that fails
more isolated music.

And worms squirm further underground,
comporting hatred toward the dawn,
while blind albino catfish weep,
augmenting what encloses them—
to hear the fluty sound, the pang
of melancholy, ageless, dim;
so live the things of night, intent
on deadened surfeit, decadent
mosaic of the muffled chords.

What is it in the darkened flush
of minus-land, the turgid come-down
thus turning stomach's inside taut
just like the warbled strokes?
Perhaps it's that the night invokes
its own embalming telephone,
a switchboard separate, sluggish, jammed
in tangled lines across the zone
of black, of being tightly sewn.

November 1982
East Palo Alto

"Diastole"

The spider formed of dewy drop
secretes in secret, invisibly,
    the glue
twixt clouds above and suicidal rain.

When thunderclouds beclap themselves in thrall
to super-building charge ethereal,
all structure turns to grey, the till to rust,
lush forests to the puffiness of canker.

They dragged us, screaming,
    from the Fundament.
And all the day that day's bleared sun did labour,
observing like a superwatchful eye—
digging, digging its way toward
the etched horizon,
where graves and new beginnings
    intersect.

November 1982
East Palo Alto

"Rise"

Action, speed the voices chimed,
like nurserymaids begrimed with mire,

  and slowly grew the room,
  with all its bobbing crew
    unreal,
  as all didst fade to indicate
the pangs of Camera's schizophrenic weal.

      Adrip with gore,
        I rose unsteady
           and
           opened
           wide
           my
           eyes.

    The kohl smeared on in crassness soothed
intense light rays, their interplay.

  In the oven of excrescence baked
  an eye so full of yeast

that inky, jet-black kohl turned blue,
  then somewhat purple in the ooze
    of melting bubbles, each the burst
      of smothered scream from any place

where Soul, buried alive, the Face
    beheld, now let's go on.

  The slick compartment tilted up—
    I rise, you rise, he rises, they

Rise, Rose, Arisen,
   must have nay been rising,
      for the sonic beam
had grown for aeons, sinkingly.

And the scream of eyes that blink now caused
the nauseating ecstasy too soon to sway
   and on the rising comet softly,
         hotly swoon.

You hear it, feel it, flash it first,
then mushroom-cloud the aftermath;

it hits you in a torrid curve
until you turn and on astonished
      crew wreak chaos
            uncontradicted,
   make Director blotchy red,—

A curtain fell and
      cut
   the world—

it cuts the fun in two.

         Deflate.

December 1982
East Palo Alto

"Collision Course"

In a land of boutiques and the swank little shops now
the time was just right for what everyone saw.

Under awnings, through cool glass embroidered with writing
now blocked-out, now flowing script,

curl'd with the barb'd hook
of elegant con-jobs, the street thus extended.

From knocking shops the hour twiddled its thumbs;
'twas midday.

The open and sun-smattered spaces shewed uniforms:
cashmere shawls, calico, fluttering plumage.

The indolent sucked on their icy, sweet popsicles;
some had the habit of traipsing about in a daze,

and Society made it all neatly connect,
but tinted pastel,
                    —why?—
                              because it would have to be.

Such was the age, and inside an emporium
moved a young girl whose slow movements were striped

with the broad strokes of licorice, much like the hair
that streamed silk-scented, smooth, straight as lace,
not a kink.

She was dangerous, was made that way, took it in stride,
like a trace of slow-acting, disguised cyanide,
but ambivalent, helpless, somehow without malice—

when a young Lord or Lady endowed with the look
that she loved—

when they passed by, or stepped in to browse,
then our young girl invited them back to the back room,

caressingly caused the brass lock to slide sideways,
pursued what she fancied, stepped out again flush'd,

and if caught in the act made her eyelashes flutter,
saying I'm not that type of a girl, if you please.

They *always* were pleas'd after that, and next door
was a dancehall where runaways danced in thin cages

to music that throbbed with what the rhythm from
ghetto-blasters pulsed with, like a newborn disease.

Down side streets to the waterfront's first advance shadows
meandered a thousand young streetkids in search

neither of icecream nor madrigal five blocks away,
as they zigzagged in circles
like everyone else just to be there,

and let the extremes
kindle bonfires, light powder-kegs—
seeping, insidious, just under the skin—

whilst our friend, the young shop girl,
kept merchandise flowing,

yes, even her blood, when from out of nowhere materialised
gamblers who suddenly—

alas, on some beastly, spontaneous pretext

—for no reason—

catching sight of her, saw the light,
and in return made her see black

as her body just lay there among the beautiful dresses,
another example as dresses turned red,

and, five shops down, the five young scientists
posed, their blood coursing, for the thrill of a group portrait
to immortalise—breathlessness.

January 1983
East Palo Alto

He plucked a deadly flower and delivered it
to his bedroom table, left it on the wood
in the sunlight's sharp, cascading theatre.

He left it centrestage in yellow trim—

shook the particles—

of dirt from off his acquiescing heel,
and shod himself in pointed shoes of felt,

with a bell on each, and donned his feather'd cap,
and stepped outside, on up, upon the street.

The Ministers were spinning webs across
from side to side, congesting normal flow
of Masquers fitted in their finery.

To the melodic buzz of sugary drones enclustred,
he snipped the sticky strands and went on through,

ajingle as he proceeded, the plumes aglow
in morning sunshine, breezes cool and dense.

He threaded back and forth, up to a throne
whereon reposed a helmeted and robed,
shield-bearing, spear-extending Queen of Dreams

whose expiation dictated that she clench
and hold the pain, the giddy stabs of sight—

he took it between the eyes, just like a Dreamer.

January 1983
East Palo Alto

"Waif"

A room with orange walls, a table chained
beneath its tray of ant-infested leavings
which stank, had been exchanged for life instead.

The layout of his mind split its corseted seams
to the whispers of its very will to live.

When he opened his mouth I used to hear the trash
that other people conned themselves, in
    breathing.

But now I only know that when he shuts
his innocent, knowing eyes the harpsichord
and all its minion counterpoint
strain tight.

No joke, he came a long way, I believe.
As everything goes right on changing with him.

January 1983
East Palo Alto

"Habitation"

No thatch adorned it, neither wool nor straw,
but rather twigs of every earthen hue,
a mix of brown and russet, all the bits
were woven as a tapestry is made,

yet powerfully, in and out, in knotted clots
of tangling underbrush whose fibres twist
amongst each other intimately, close.

Betimes it filtered moisture from the sky,
each droplet searched and run exactingly
through networks of inscrutable design.

In time of drought its dusty, thirsting sweep
of fine-twined convolution, snaking threads,
gave no smell whatsoever, nor a feel
for what it really was—

to breathe it in
a lighted spark was needed, plus the streak
of well-aimed motion gently, gently
nudged.

January 1983
East Palo Alto

"Mandelstam Street"

When walking down the street you find no truth,
but only clinging cotton-candy strands

which bind your limbs and gum your eyelashes
to cancerise the world with nothingness,

then offhand I should've thought you're on the wrong
street—maybe never to find the right one—

die in suffocation underneath
the smiles they waft, but just remember this:

Your life in its rightness or wrongness assumes a street
that's right for you—never mind that it's concealed,

and though you never find it, isn't it true
your street is simply waiting there for you?

January 1983
East Palo Alto

"Sore Throat"

I stepped off the bus and felt the dusk air.

Sometimes the air can be so terribly cruel,
so much more terrible in its invisibility.

Sinuous fingers of night air,
blinking their razour-lidded eyes,
stroked my swollen, stinging
throat that stays alive somehow
by swallowing,

rent by knives, as though
ripped out like that of a sheep
first espied from afar by the
soft-skulking
predator.

February 1983
East Palo Alto

"Flying"

My fiancée said she'd come by aeroplane
though I begged her to reconsider,

the train being so very much more
suited to our kind.

Trains are like licorice whips
    which the Three Fates
        spin, measure,
    and snip.

Once, from such a fast-moving
    window I saw a thundercloud
assuming the intimate oracles
    of shape and perspective,
    an enigma more oblique and
self-contained with
    each mutation.

That's, I think, why
she chose to fly—

to go through it rather than
    beneath—

She must know how
        bullets feel—

I know what they pierce.

February 1983
East Palo Alto

"World View"

When my only friend in the world
took me for all I was worth,

I must confess, it gave my stomach
a queer little turn,

treated me to a blunt-edged
but lightning-fast jolt
that felt more like a
whip-lash than anything else.

It made me a little colder,

a trifle more slow in nailing
my thick rubbery lips
to another's cheek—

however enticing
its axiomatic deliciousness.

Now I seem to see composition
in place of colours,

at least some of the time.

February 1983
East Palo Alto

"Dead End #23"

Everyone's twisted like a pretzel.

I've seen your indestructible eye,
swollen tearduct still dry,

become the loveliness of a crystal
shot-glass flying through the despair

 just before it smashes on
the chipped hearth of
a fireplace full of cold ashes.

Help me, I'm sad.

Well have I earned the right to talk with you,
or must I go back and try once again

to get it down on paper?

February 1983
East Palo Alto

"Mitosis"

A pack of swag-bellied scavengers
squealing in passage
  made me one of them,
our pain bubbling up
through the scum in
frantic dissonant yelps.

The motionless grey walls
resembled a curtain of smoke

that only the echoing surfaces
of my formlessness could contain.

My clanging eardrums out-shouted
their own little pinpricks
of warning as I opened up,
tried to turn myself
inside out, and
    divided.

Now there were
  two of me.

I almost understood life.

February 1983
East Palo Alto

She did not tell her husband
that she no longer needed him.

Grease sizzled, most explosively
spattering sensitive skin,
the longer left to fry on the
licking of a gas-flame.

I smile encouragement as if
to tell you it's a hard
smash-up you face.

Peace be with you, gentle
sister, may the traces dissolve.

March 1983
East Palo Alto

"Let's Go Dancing"

The ball of her heel explodes
because I lit a fuse there.

She comes crashing down
breaking the exquisite neck
that drives me crazy,
sends me flitting on my powdery wings
into the flame.

In the crick of her neck—
in the ball of my heel—
in the stump of a botched amputation—

someone slipped
iron filings of death in his afternoon tea,

recycled now as the stern iron blood
  driving *driving*
her back and forth across the dance-floor—
my stern iron tormentor.

March 1983
East Palo Alto

"Dialectic of Self-Perception"

Sit over there.
Not here. Not near me.

Spat upon like the village clown,
you wonder how mid the knives of the world
you ever loved them,

the beautiful ones, the vision
which makes you, even now, grit your teeth
and hold it, searing, in arms of steel,

frying yourself to an overdone crisp,
inedible, unwanted rag-doll
flapping away your double-jointed life,

tossing yourself like the thing
you thought you were like, but
in actuality, have turned out to
   be.

April 1983
East Palo Alto

"Lisa's Story"

Sometimes disgust
surpasses pity,

especially when its pulsing
aneurysm of a cause
does not directly concern one.

Like when that fellow of no consequence,
as recounted third-hand,
saw his lover wallowing
in debauchery after debauchery
and called her mother

who flew out like an avenging fury
only to stomach the syrupy lies
of that painted automaton of her blood—

and fly back just as impotently.

I can hear the girl calling
her hopelessly similar, empty
paramour and sweetly, on
overdrive, cooing
Good-bye.

April 1983
East Palo Alto

"Reflections"

Crystal doors fly open,
    disgorging
  a mass of
quivering, translucent jelly.

The Glass, the Glass—
    they all approach it—
    assorted bits of frippery—

tormented people, who to escape
    all harm
have made an iron-clad pact
with Looking-Glass's frigid,
smooth, and ambidextrous
      symmetry.

Ah well, the Lady
    her lustrous hair
  stops combing when the Glass
      decrees,

and down the corridor
      a slave
slaveringly licks the
  Diadem with all its
    streaks of jeweled grime.

His eyes will flicker
  to the degree that
    Looking-Glass sees fit to
slam down hard upon his
  precious feeling.

Ah, the Rebirth
stirs anew.

And now a little Swedish girl
fresh off the street
    catches a glimpse
of all her fragile imperfections,
now collapsing on the floor
    astonished.

When she awakes they all
will throng and welcome her
unto the place which,

love or hate, she
cannot flee.

Some shapes get sticky
pressed between the spate
of slippery leaves
    but at least
they somehow care about
    their warping.

All of them exchange
    degrees of warmth,
        degrees of being
            strange.

May 1983
East Palo Alto

I took steps along a path of ice.
Others aped me.
They moved, at variance with one another.
They spent heat and movement.
White mist escaped the nostril.

Rollers glided.

I climbed the stairs.
I went into my house and, again, the un-wanting
   enfolded me.

My stem leads to the corner, flowering
in sheets of supple weave.
The cushions are soft; they give way gently,
easefully sheathed in a skin the colour of
soft, unwalked upon snow.

When I take my lying, the lank hair, around back,
is smothered but does not die;
when I turn to see the wall my ear
is pressed flat but is not crushed.

At night the brightness shines through, and I feel it
reflected in my eyes as I lie to the glance paralysed,
unsleeping but peaceable.

I watched it make a bar of light across the coverlet.
I felt the beads of glistening moisture, the cheek burning.
I felt the great distance from which my feet
pressed hard against the wood.

Pressing, relaxing.

October 1983
Stanford

"Intergalactic Exigencies"

Hovering, equidistant,
betwixt the various, vaunted points of exile,
she tasted of the Inner Orbits, tried
the planetoid virginity of Io,

moved farther out, and turned her fickle gaze
to a churning sea of molten glass, beheld
the transitory colours.
Opposite,

the sun lay dazzlingly apart, and streamed
in sullen brilliance, like a million flashes
thrown into the Bowl of Seeing, but mixt with—
belief.

February 1984
Stanford

53

"Kozmic Blues"

To-morrow's shattered pieces
like ice inside the skull.

Bitter hatred smashed a decaying, empty dream.

The ambulance flashed its bright
 revolving
   light-screams,
a flimsy thrill of death entwined the sighing.

The frozen clouds release a choking torrent
which drenches with a penetrating chill;

its suffocating mesh of clinging needles
freezes the breath
to ice-cubes
that crack and split from within.

How long can an armour of welts
     protect the mind—
   keeping its agony-sugar
       undissolved?

February 1986
New York City

"Inheritance"

The whips of yesterday
shred To-day's dainty flesh.

I would abruptly fall to my knees
with a hollow-cracking sound

if only enough of my listeners
understood the acoustics.

February 1986
New York City

i.

That one is different from
all the other young heiresses,
cause she weeps bucketfuls
  of sweat in place of tears.

Can you believe it, that crying
could be that much work, or
  whatever?

ii.

Similarly the most
  beautiful girls
are often tempted to
make themselves ugly, and
then cry, cause they can't.

The beautiful can do anything—
  except not exist.

March 1986
New York City

"Bedtime"

      i.

He glided up the stairs
like smoke dissolving.

Carouse below continued
while the night
exhaled the stale cliché
whose sad-eyed death
  extinguishes the
embers in a breath.

      ii.

It's late beyond all telling.
  Come to bed.
You've seen enough,
  the comedy is
    dead.

May 1986
New York City

i never quite fit in,
but let's form the cross anyway.

kind stranger, please stand
over there in the brightness;

elizabeth—under the vaulted arch;
you, my dear, in the cage; and

  svetlana, by the far wall
where the light stops,
near the razour.

i'll stand in the centre and
  hold it for a thousand years
if necessary—

now all we need is jesus christ,
  and some pain.

June 1986
New York City

"Suicide"

i am going to kill myself.
why am i going to kill myself?
because i don't have a girlfriend.
why don't i have a girlfriend?
because i am ugly.
why am i ugly?
because i believe myself to be ugly.
why do i believe myself to be ugly?
because the other children spat on me.
why did they do this?
because i was different.
why was i different?
because i wanted to kill myself.

July 1986
New York City

i.

thick lashes provocatively droop,
forging an invisible, but unbreakable, chain.

lips burn for a taste of fire:
a vacuum straddling fang-divided darkness.

life's a subtile masque; the gleaner rakes
  its chill, decaying stubble;
the unbursting surface
stretches tissue-thin
the faded glimpse.

ii.

being dies, and dying crawls;
the crashing staff will scarcely
strike, but whistle in the
stinging arc by
which it im-
potently
falls.

August 1986
New York City

death as personified by the
Elizabethans must be a thing
much like my self—morbid
  yet very fashion-conscious.
and yet i've seen members of
my family die a slow death
and i know, from my observations,
that this thing's entire force
lies in its opposition to
  personality.

August 1986
New York City

"The Stench of Schenectady"

Ironshod,
bound in greaves,
I clank as I stagger,
my armour resplendent
in the cauliflower sun.

The unwed sky is so
purple with swollen gout
that no cloud dares adorn
its puffy surface.

Dead, corpses pay unto the
debt-collector
  obeisance, and just remember—
if it should swell too far,
upwelling from its aerial abode,
then will the sun descend slowly,
crushing us, like a battleship,
as it sinks.

August 1986
New York City

"Sodium"

You can feel the
   red
hysteria seething
within a piece of itself.

The swelling tongue
would float on draughts of
  laughter-stench
that would have
    bled
through rotting carrion-pustules
to escape the spreading burst
of slurping, sharp-edged
grief which like a razour
slices to the bone.

All feeling bloats;
I haven't overfed my
in-sobbed throbs of strife,
but will Decrease
their daily bread in the
interests of hysteria—
should I shrivel or explode?

September 1986
New York City

"Lighter Than Air"

She weakens imperceptibly and crashes
most horribly, picks up her broken limbs,
and calmly starts to fall apart, though calm
less so in spirit than outwardly to view.

From under the skin dull cramps and stabs
    cause panic,
overload the system,
      executioners.

Like an addict she joins the queue;
it snakes its way
so slowly,
an inch at a time,
  towards the Brink--

in her x-ray imaginings she has a view
of all the Drag, the icy, probing lights
that animate it and, of course, the Fear.

Searing red and blue, the electric prick of cubes
that mutate into different things at once,
it flickers indistinctly in the Losing--

whilst cars hiss by, propelled of energy
ever made to dance in jagged, fading streaks,
and gentle, suction-sculpted stars rain down,
sticky to rough, and lavender to brown.

She rises till her forehead scrapes the heavens
and, scraping, teaches Heaven how to bleed.

September 1986
New York City

Our murderer reclined
 on a throne of frozen
blood and clapped bracelets
to see the slavering painted
mirage of sweet tenderness
opening so wide as to
    swallow itself and
  vanish in a squelching flash.

From either side he, the
fanaticism, I mean, of our
lives is
  maintained by trembling
statues of powdery siftage
which trained apes of
silver tint
  must perpetually
mould and reshape.

It seems a trapdoor that only
the smoky-voiced enigma
now performing
can fall between
the starved lips of which—
  to what degree, regarding
our own sawdust-
stuffed entrails,
melodious, famished,
suggestive?

September 1986
New York City

"Requiem"

Care weaves a mask, but in the dark
all darkness is invisible.

So consummate the twain their tryst,
  the tryst its lopside, seeming twain,
the both of them in streams of moon
aglow with luminescence.

She brings herself, in dead of
    Night,
        to unspeakable, shuddering
            Requiem.

September 1986
New York City

"Breaking Down"

rustle of papers
fifth period, seventh grade—
darkest depth of hell.
winter 1976.
dying.

heavy-lidded tears like
beads of blue ice—
teacher why don't you
look up, why won't you
see what is happening?

the divorce—we have no money.
fear.

please.
don't break,
not now.

oh please, heavy-lidded
like beads of ice
i can feel them coming,
on the brim,
no please
heavy-lidded they drop.

please stop.
before they see—
just give it back to me,
see, my mind is
cracking like
ice.

nudges, giggling
all around me,
the contemptuous whispers.

breaking down
has to be the loneliest
feeling on earth.

October 1986
New York City

"Men and Women"

Women seem to have a strange
'affinity' for men.
  I have a weakness.
For women.

Disgust as well but pro-
  portionately toward
men more than women
(women make me stupid,
weak in the knees)—

perhaps I hate the men because
they succeed so incredibly
(rather than the women
for *letting* them succeed,
letting them destroy me
so utterly, so completely).

From sunup to sundown
I'm on display,
proselytising,
preaching an abstinence

that comes across as
Self-hatred.

October 1986
New York City

"Acid"

Being around her at last
has become

too corrosive, too acrid,

an ecstasy of unleaded saccharine
searing the skin,

taking off the finish,

exposing my weakness like it's
never been exposed,—

making my love bleed
in bright little
  bubbles.

October 1986
New York City

it was so sad.

the child never got a summation—
kicked off like a pustulous dog,

and i'm writing
    about it.

and, of course, I'm trying
to get a passport
out of here.

this country is a potato.

stop laughing at me, the
    insanity

was left on my doorstep

by a passel of swag-bellied
scavengers, pranksters, thieves,

and philanthropists.

October 1986
New York City

I can see the dead,
oh g-d can't you see them?

they fill the world—
  they extend as far as
the eye can see,

heaped packed clawing
for space.

cracked lips, empty sockets.

jesus, i'm losing it,

throwing up my
sanity all over the

humpbacked flagstones.

October 1986
New York City

"Antonym"

I am a slave,
  I am a thing
left in the gutter
as a sting
to pierce the brittlest hoof or heel
or shoe or serviceable wheel
new-forged of steel
without the strength to,
having weakened,
strongly
feel.

November 1986
New York City

"Reinventing the Greenhouse"

Warm water smells of snow—
the snow from which it melted.

In summertime beneath the shade
of budding trees all in a line
whose rotten leaves last autumn fell
and now from a grave of mud divine
that life goes on, the roses smell
not quite the same
but emanate their quickening
fragrance as a bruise
beneath the skin
  oozes
the purple flush in vain,
since bleeding never
helped much.

In time the ground will slake itself
under torrents of the choking rain,
but who will drive
  the hogs to market,
who will rediscover pain?

November 1986
New York City

I'm all I have—is that a sin,
or should I hate myself and die?

Should I scald
  my hand in an oven
smoking in a loathsome
ditch which though it
used to be a master-
  piece of mud is
now a slough of
slimy puddles
    full of vermin,
        irredeemable, a
            scar?

Every month or so
  a Star
shines palest crimson
in the sky and gives
the upward-glancing eye
a receptacle of strength,

streaking with fire the rivulet
on a lover's unkissed cheek.

November 1986
New York City

I can sense the sub-harmonic spasms
trapped underneath your tinsel-plated
squeaky-clean loquacity—

Despair
turns thinking inward
where the centre, too dense for light and air,
is like a subterranean spider,
patient, blind, seductive.

November 1986
New York City

"Degrees"

Degrees extend so far beyond the dull horizon's
    jutting brow—
so far beyond all horizontal parallelisms of Soul—
that, far as you go,
there's always more—
always a tepid cataclysm—
all through the grades of being alive
    divided grossly, lopsidedly.

Maybe someday another person will make a mistake
and actually find me deserving of a second glance.

Or murder,
in the first degree.

November 1986
New York City

"Definition"

Snug,
I slept oblivious to the storm,
  its livid workmanship, the frightful kiss
that hailstone, indiscriminate, bestowed.

  Midnight embers
hissed the tallied cost
of tempest-broken stem and battered tree;
  their gaseous oracle, half-throbbingly,
  though soporific,
screened off to the side,
    arose and smote
from smouldering pangs of ash.

Nursemaid woke me, Charles and Marianne
   already risen,—
 greedily we fell
to breakfast, strawberries ripe the giddy fare,
and as we ate, their juices burst apart
inside our youthful mouths,
        and at the point
where lip meets lip (in wanton kiss or, better,
disjoint anatomy) all wetness seemed
to pierce the framework,
  only growing wetter
as crimson welled therefrom and off the chin
did drip to plate, in morsels re-absorbed
  for richer chewing;
        Nanny saw, deplored,
and scolded mess made messier by the lack
of any fork for spearing or a spoon
whose curvature would keep from being spilt
(at random) flesh encapsulated, moulded

by loving metal, but, alas, our house
were far too poor for silverware—
    Papa
kept servants first—but Madame Gleb had died,
so now we might obtain it;
    governess
dead (burial at noon), we stepped outside
away from cook and nursemaid whispering.

The lawn was strewn with
        shattered flecks of hail,
 and viscous mud squelched underfoot;
    grey earth
all soggy, with scree admixt and bits of flotsam,
extended, beyond the hedges, shapelessly.

January 1987
New York City

"All I Can Do"

Slice back the sky
to find a heart of stone—
lick it til your tongue bleeds
til your dreams die
like little grey ducks caught
in an oil slick
which spills from a ruptured
hull of sky-blue steel.

The crashing sea will drown
its wide-eyed worshippers
sooner than free them
to fall in love with the
mother of all they are.

Never before was
the chisel of love
more electrically piercing—
it makes the air
flash to your strobe-sight
like the skin of a
life-dinghy's life-giving wood
gathers barnacles
on the blood-hungry strand
whose teeth are the jagged rocks
of my pain
  whose eyes are the moist red
anemones of my unsub-
stantiated floating
love-mist.

Beautiful One, you know the sky
you feel oh god
the things i feel.

Your hair is like the sunlight
from your sun-throne mind—
it shines beautifully
with such a swim
of unreflected quicksand—
i think my dying has
never felt so pleasant:
to drown in your eyes,
to eat your invisible breath
and dream at night of the lungs
which spilled them,
awake a corpse,
still go on with a frozen
heart—i love you so.

How is it possible?—
to overpave your footsteps
with interconnecting
sighs of hard-pressed heat
which surround you,
press round warm and invisible,
that is all I can do.

February 1987
New York City

81

"The House That Dripped Blood"

When I came to you with my tears
you told me to go to Hell.

Why did you tell me this?

I found there that the
mountains ooze an unstoppable
heaviness of spirit.

The clouds rain a perpetual
stream of tears,
emptying themselves on
whomever stops, with a sigh,
slowly to die in his tracks.

There was a church dripped blood,
I went inside,
there was a dead woman in the cellar,
I hanged myself beside her.

Suspended, our corpses face to face,
I think we felt a little
easier in the grave
listening to the ghosts,
letting go.

Emptiness gnawed at us
like a rat left in
  a cat-less granary,
sharp little teeth biting,
soft little feet pattering
amongst the rotting
bottles of acid—

and facing her cold dead eyes
I saw myself and needed no eyes.

Through the grate I needed no ears
to hear the clear squeak of
the engine grinding souls.

I needed no mind to see my
life ground to powder
and carried away by the
hot dry wind which
asphyxiates all hope and dignity,
any memory of you,
any value you had as a person—

Hanging there I became you.

Welcome to Hell.

February 1987
New York City

"Paul's Girlfriend"

She rides the bus home to Utopia
amidst a shower of sharp
love sickles and razour-blossoms,
mirror blind-sight
  head-on
    from behind—
the seeing sears all round
  from every angle,
    inside out,
rare precious scented stuff
you lock away
it hurts so badly, boxes
within boxes, locks of such
cat's-eye intricacy
you'll forget the
Secret and lose her
right in the eye
of your raging storm of love,
  iron winds, raging waves
battering the fish-eye crags
which never shut, never
    yield.

In the morning she
  takes the bus to work—
do you stop to think what she's
doing away from you,
  moment to moment,
away from your love—
is the lock strong enough?
Do the swarms of suspicion
twist up the fibre of your mind,
do they rob you of sleep

like a thief in the night
who slips a secret drug deep
in the blood,
  or do you let it be,
content with her beauty
and unafraid of life's equations—

Are you pleased with yourself?

March 1987
New York City

"Enchantment"

Purple waves generate
white sea-spray against
a dull orange dawn.

On the far horizon's verge
a slow surge of pink light
bleeds mysteriously from the
rising Chrysanthemum.

With skin light as ozone,
a single delicate grey vein,
the delicate supple hand
is rising, iron-handedly,
languid.

The intricate chrome-grey sting
from its innermost chamber
discharges a piercing capsule,
an enchanting 9-gram kiss.

Glistening red wine
trickles to slake
the sand's tawny
thirst.

April 1987
New York City

"Cracking It"

You have to crack the past open
like a recalcitrant shinbone.

The fear.
A new school.
A new schoolyear.

According to certain eminently respectable researchers
the persecuted child sticking out like a sore thumb
is more or less the 'architect' of his or her own
dih-fickle-ties.

I knever new I was an Arkitect.

Lips lisping.
The lips of a sadist.
Articulating endearments to the effect that I made him
sick, and was a fucking queer.

The highland park 'independent' school district,
1974.

February 1989
Dallas

"Forgive, Maybe—Forget, Never"

Stephen Bartholow, repulsive.
His fishnibbled sockets
gaze up through the freezing opacity
at hulls in passage. I blew his
brains out in Petrazavodsk,
put a millstone round the neck and
dumped him

before the first thin sheets of ice
began to spread outwards, thickening
beneath the gigantic motionless
pale red shape in the sky
like the cyanide
requisitioned for Mark Drinkwater's
slice of the wedding cake they all,
sooner or later, come back
to feed upon.

Laura Chandler's valentine's day
chocolates were similarly laced
with a bitter-tasting
vertigo—the glass tabletop
cracked under the impact. A fly settled
on the bridge of her nose. Rubbing
its front legs and dipping down
to drink of the salty tearducts
before they filmed over.

I have to stop now.
Forgive me.

March 1989
Dallas

"Black Hundreds"

Some stopped their ears by gulping down the grog
of folklore: ghosts and witches.

Creek to creek,
the counties held a breakage of opinion.

As long, dry, tawny grasses bend and ripple
in afternoon extension of the dawn,
the Old and Young alike give up their dead
and talk about it openly.

Some doubt,
while others find the cosmic chain in chaos,
disorder strewing shredded leaves to carpet
the squelching bog, but portals say it best,
say to the world, as to a patient naked:

For awhile there,
no one knew if you would make it.

March 1990
Dallas

"You Can't Go Back"

A dissipating puff of carbon monoxide
drifts above the factory chimneys,
seeking the smokestack which belched it forth—

we all of us need a mother's love,
seeking what none of us understand.

March 1990
Dallas

We have novels, elaborate alibis, to construct.
Storefronts. My mind is full of
Uptown right now.

Uptown sickness.

Frederick Douglass Boulevard.
Adam Clayton Powell.
Lenox Avenue.

Like arteries branching and snaking
across the chest of a corpse.

Heading towards 5th and 110th,
I came across a wedding reception.

Several bridesmaids, grinning little girls,
their whole lives in front of them,
resplendent in satin.

March 1999
New York City

"Circling the Drain"

I have feelings inside me
bustling, jostling, coming together,
coalescing, fusing, breaking apart.

No, never.
Yes, someday.
Not once in my lifetime.

Come again, go away?
How can I have a lover when no one wants to be friends?
I never make the grade, always trip, always fumble.

She seldom answers
my neverending stream of bothersome tripe.

We have to reco'nise the sad fact that
she may not be in'erested.

Maybe so.
Probably not.

But there it is.
You have to look reality square in the face.

January 2000
New York City

Learn wisdom.
Inhale the bitter fragrance
from a brazier of soot-blackened bronze:
That was then, this is now.

The wolves at Council Rock were correct:
who wants a pile of bones
licked clean long ago?

She can cavort with whomever she pleases,
consigning us to the unmarked grave
where ex-lovers get dumped.

Learn wisdom.
A thorn-brake of sharp-edged brambles
can enclose the deadliest drifting nightshade.
Be glad of the scratches,
rejoice in the runaway freight train swerving to
annihilate someone else, for a change.

Learn wisdom.
Remember, as the child remembers,
setting aside resentment,
pouring out the cup of poison
before thirst overcomes us.

September 2005
Dallas

See the two of them.

Take a ball of spikes and
nail your two hands together,
holding the pain.

Whether it's right
or wrong,

whether you were born to feel this,
or destined to take up a battle-axe and
lop off heads right and left,

blood seeps, drop by drop.
Life courses, pain thrums and thrills
from the buds and leaflets, quickening, opening,
till every pebble and blossom exhales the chorus:

g-d damn her.

g-d damn her forever.

September 2005
Dallas

"Under the Pole Star"

A towering cliff of ice,
monolithic, unstoppable,
sheds avalanche-like accumulations of hoarfrost,

shearing down toward the sea,
slowly, at its own pace, uprooting and gouging,
as the tightfisted, grinding totality
crushes homesteads and hills.

We gulped the icy stinging sleet
streaming down from the freezing lead-coloured clouds,

slashed and pricked by a subterranean hunger—
a hunger that never stops grinding.

I gave my fur-lined reversible jacket
to a shivering wretch.

Too late repenting of such incomprehensible,
imbecilic generosity, enraged,
I shot my toe off with a steel-tipped harpoon.

I mutilated myself (for having hacked off my toe—
for being one stroke from footlessness,
two hops down the bloody plank
from one-leggedness).

Adrift on the iceflow of kinless adversity,
I read the stars and made me a compass.

Life is bitter, but also rich,
but most of all incomprehensible.

Keen-edged pain ominously smoulders
in the beautiful flickering of the hardhearted stars.

August 2006
Dallas

"Allison"

She glides past
like water seeking an outlet –
like ice so slippery you'll break your scruffy neck
on its diamond-like sheen.

Her fearsome impassivity
trifles with your soul
the way a small child
tries to disassemble some flashy
dimestore tiara.

Reactive, she falls in love
the way an Addict falls down
a flight of steps,
in slow motion.

Unable to gauge her own
perfect-ness,
defining herself
the way a blind scientist
extrapolates an extinct monster
from the one surviving thighbone
handed down for generations,
from mother to daughter—

Like a tuning fork blasted by lightning,
transmogrified into something new and unique,
she supersedes herself, loves
like she takes her next breath—

just like the Lungfish
because, in the chill mud of Becoming,
she must.

February 2007
Dallas

"Romance of the Rose"

It's time to shrill from the stricture of trumpets
the earsplitting arpeggios disguising themselves
as a laboured expectoration of sputum—

Like a compound of vinegar with frothing nectar
distilled from a mixture of honey and blood—

the throat dries out and parches
to remember her Life-quenching kisses—

Her name?
A secret the Rose petals keep.

February 2007
Dallas

"Life and Death in the Stone Age"

Two of the tribe's rising youth
were drowned in the crashing irresistible surge.

Every time a moss-colored flame
leaps against the horizon,

brayings and pipings desultorily weave
a collective but fast-fading dirge

that plays itself out with the passage
of repetitive days and meaningless,
mind-numbing nights.

Hethrej, more dead than alive,
babbles, in his delirium, of the flood driving
all before it, the vast incoming tide
with its whirlpools and spouts of spray
hemmed in by the granite cliffs, flimsy coracles
broken to bits in the surge.

I stood there, looking down,
at what was left of Quithlunc.

His gaping sockets were empty,
his bracelets disarranged by the current,
his naked fishnibbled body
cast up on the strand.

I recognised Embla
from the pallour of her inimitable cheekbones;
gone was the pleasing flush of girlhood
colouring her irresistible face, setting
off her light blue eyes,

filling her lips with warm vividness,
tart like spiced wine.

It felt like a thousand-ton sledgehammer
that fails to annihilate on the first down-stroke,
the head full of blinding, colliding comets
and deafening topheavy clangour.

Death always muddies the understanding,
bangs the gavel down with a sharp enough
cracking impact

that we forget everything but the sound itself,
ignoring what the sound originally
was supposed to signify,

spurning everything, even the victims,
in our stubborn determination

to play with concepts
we don't yet understand.

March 2008
Dallas

"Things That Hurt"

Universal suffrage with its webbed fingers and toes
paddles the listing skiff of State,
emits fluidly legato hiccoughs of bubbling
tightfisted
agony.

Helpful chambermaids
immolate themselves.

The wooden wattle-daubed structures,
half cathedral, half wigwam,
scream as flames lick the wind.

Lady Lushington advanced,
hem trailing as the train dragged
over flagstones impregnated
with shoots of blistering whortleberry,
smooth-budded whin.

All the town knows
what the great fictive claw-handled monster
shrieks on seeing,
falls backward,
careening, falling down hard.

Self-preservation bids us bury
the gem-encrusted treasures of language,
enameled cups and trenchers filled with glittering
word-hoards, conundrums of
multiple meaning.

Ideas are cold.
Intellection is dry as dust,

empty as a camouflaged snakeskin.

Things that hurt sometimes come close:

intimacy,
incest,
quadrilaterals,

subterfuge.

March 2008
Dallas

Dissonant rhymes push against each other,
blur boundaries, dissolve the linkages
preordaining some poetic collision;

opposites no longer attract.

Pre-eminent as dust pouring through the isthmus of some
lopsided hourglass,

a world-famous, crenelated stanza
sharpened on the whetstone of infinity
slices almost too deep,
nicking consciousness,
making changes in the way
people perceive themselves,

too beautiful to be endured,
or perhaps too invidious?

March 2008
Dallas

"Balance"

The amplification
of a word shouted forth
as from the mouth of a cannon
puffs me up with a strange weightlessness,
germinating outwards, swallowing the entire universe.

The crowbar makes love to the scourge,
the Crook and the Flail commit
indiscretions condensing like the topheavy
hanging globulous droplets
ready to break and rain down,
waterlogging the porous dry earth.

All things hang together, the more inert
the more turreted—
crenelated like the false battlement
incubating the inside of what was either a dream,
a false memory,
or (t)ruth.

March 2008
Dallas

"The Human Tendency to Rationalise"

He stumbled in midstride,
just sort of broke apart, like a popsicle melting.

There was cunning,
slipperyshifting forgetfulness
and chiseled meanness, ripplyrunning,

but most of all there was Oath-breaking.

Greta was softly laughing as she wept,
her tears mixed of honey and blood,
intoxicating, thirst-slaking.

I wept for the sins
against which I fitted and measured my blunt-edged capacity
always to do the wrong thing.

March 2008
Dallas

"Away with Words"

I've snatched a handful of your
prickly-stemmed rose-petal names,
strewing them to the night breeze
the way you asphyxiated me
a finger at a time clamped
round the throat.

Too much of anything can tilt the mechanism,
strike the solar plexus so hard
you literally see stars
in that last glittering instant.

That's why some of us tend to avoid
what we can't get a handle on,
can't define and thus
cut down to our own miniscule size.

Do you know what it feels like to rip a newborn
thought from the womblike subconscious
before the midwife of compromise has
watered it down?

Nightmares come not just in the small hours,
not just when the sun has gone down.

Just look at yourself sometime—
fling the door open and throw yourself
in front of the glass
without giving your own terrible, inescapable
crimes and shortcomings a chance
to make themselves over.

March 2008
Dallas

"Scraping the Surface"

Re-used (like the dram of juice
squeezed from a lemon),
reconstituted (through the bilge of transfiguration),
reason prates of
a trapezoidal tumescent relief, whispers
to pull yourself together.

But the precious lifesbloood
is both deaf and
adulterated.

In between the stewpots women
compare notes, dispute, wrangle, and caucus.

In the flickering embers of late-night casuistry
the children that we used to be snuggled,
sucking our thumbs.

April 2008
Dallas

Darkness blankets the land.

A burning bush levitates,
sprinkling phosphorescent smouldering
twigs and bits of radioactive bracken
all over the place.

A beacon of sorts the Sybil called it
before slashing her own throat with a pair
of rusted scissors—the violence of the deed
(she practically decapitated herself)
took me aback.

So now it comes down to me—
the only surviving acolyte Shaman—
when Strektha iced herself
the whole fucking picture disintegrated,
level playing fields up-ended themselves,

forests abdicated
leaving just a collection of branches
bearded with thick hanging moss—
tangles of suffocating, pathless, trackless
undergrowth that goes on forever.

Should we migrate, and risk starving to death,
or stay too long in one place,
offering ourselves up to the marauding outlaws
that creep silently in the dark, shadowing us,
gathering strength?

Her dreams foretold the future,
governed our movements,
made us feel safe.

What now, the Elders ask me?
I haven't the slightest idea what to do;

the words I try to come up with
are stillborn, deformed.

How can I tell them the truth:
daybreak is peeking over the mountains.
It's time to start blundering in the harsh
blinding light.

April 2008
Dallas

"Mating Season"

His eyes flicker and burn in the dark
  seeking miracles,
burning holes in what they transpierce
the way a candle sears its way through
a thin film of gauze.

Relics of burnished, handed-down beadwork
remind us of tribal duties, collective responsibilities.

In his burning lust he traces
the girl's face, the girl's shoulders, subsumed
on a mound of smouldering charcoal
such as woodcutters, squatting round it
and rubbing their callused, chapped hands,
seem to be worshipping.

Can you see, between the dimly perceived trees, in the mist,
the shape of the Woman, hovering like a fleet-footed gazelle,
ready to dematerialise in a burst of slippery
almost magical quickness?

All around us the men are dying of a sickness
that none can define, few can even pronounce.

And now, the mating season finishes
what idle daydreams began.

The work of the tribe languishes
like an ill-made garment shucked off by the wayside.

Too busy for thoughts of survival,
no longer gathering grain and skins for the winter,
I join the others, in search of rough bliss.

Thoughts of self-preservation
are like the bits of clothing I burn to pluck
from her supple, smooth, unblemished,
firm flesh.

April 2008
Dallas

"Perfect Love"

What she wanted was not quite the same thing
as what he wanted—
they cancel'd each other out—
contradicting the very essence of what it means
to bridge differences.

He wanted what all boyfriends want.

She wanted to feel loved, to feel the strength of
his strong, safe, unconditional love.

I wanted for each of them not to get hurt.

He begged her, but she'd never done it before.
She was afraid, and hesitated.

He turned up the pressure, threatening
to go elsewhere, using rejection
as a sort of impalpable weapon.

I saw the hurt in her eyes, the wavering,
a spirit at war with itself.

Looking into the scared eyes of her swain
I saw through the swagger and artifice; I saw the fear,
the need, the deadly necessity to prove himself
not just in her eyes, but all the more, in his own.

To my half-surprise, I saw that he loved her with
a true and deep love.

A demon perched astride his fourteen-year-old shoulders
whispered mind-bending lies, and cast seeds in the

barren soil of monstrously denuded self-worth.

Theirs had started out as the perfect love story.

Variables crystallised weaving lattices
of flexibility, keeping out the night breeze.

White tapers glistened from floor to ceiling,
hissing, flickering, whispering in their
changeless radiance of lives gone astray.

Simplicity most always hurts.

Truth (and what is truth, if not painful?)
lives (and thrives) in simplicity.

Where the thing called 'love' resides—
who can whisper its address
and retain a straight face?

April 2008
Dallas

"Conflagration"

The groin of the ceiling was creased like an invisible
loudspeaker amplifying the hiss of the flames.

Crackling speech dancing like tongues of blistering heat
conjures the salamander whose shimmering scales
hover just out of reach, edges blurring,
words and sentences running together;

everything shifts, reverberates,

as the fire licks its flickering fangs and bicuspids,
biding its time, pacing itself, crouching
to vault to the other side of the street.

May 2008
Dallas

Fan the stars one at a time.
Some flicker and glimmeringly
wink before going out
in the dark.

People sometimes go out
like a tiny quivering flame.

Look deep in their eyes
and perhaps
you won't find anything.

May 2008
Dallas

"Elfrida"

A black wimple concealed
what was left of her hair.

The white face somehow scarcely seemed human,
detachable like a visor of deafness and blindness.

What was she thinking as she filled
the cup with red liquid,
controlling the slightest movement
of one who lurked in the shadows,
daring those who came after
to build on her work, to perfect what she started
in destroying posterity?

It's such a strange, strange way to live.

Such a bitter pledge--her stepson, the boy king,
stabbed in the back, slumping forward on a galloping horse,
fighting unconsciousness, a constricting pain in the groin
shooting like a star of ill-omened futurity.

Never again shall her womb span the sides of the
irreconcilable.

Aethelred was the last.
Redeless, accurst.

Crimes which can never be forgotten cry out for redress.

May 2008
Dallas

I knew a girl eschewed compromise;

all I wanted was the soft unknowable bliss of her touch—
she wanted more out of life; it was her desire
that the starving be fed, that children with AIDS
be given medicines free of charge—

before her Awakening (as she called it)
all she cared about was how her hair looked.

Once she prepared a sort of all-purpose broth,
trying to nurse me back to health
(I'd slipped on a banana peel
outside her front door).

Little did she imagine
the feelings painted into a corner of my mind,
bunched up like some infection
besieged by white blood cells,
half sheepish, half snarling—

I hated her for making me look at myself.

June 2008
Dallas

"Turtle Creek Boulevard"

It was a house
standing at what felt like the epicenter of madness
with stealthy, creaking noises for those who knew how
to listen.

Listen hard enough, and you can hear
the dead discoursing on the sins of the living.

He feared ghosts,
but also loved, and respected, them.

He wanted to become one with them,
not yet realising
that nothing on this earth
has ever been more inevitable.

His mother chided him for fidgeting as they
both lay there, pretending to sleep,
waiting for the man of the house
to come home and begin protecting them
from the things that lurk in dark corners.

Every time a car glided past on the road outside,
every time some late-night salesman
drove past, the tyres of his jalopy
making a hissing sound on the pavement,

the headlights in passing projected
a luminous ghost on the ceiling of their upstairs bedroom.

They say at the very end your whole life flashes past.

He looked up at lives gliding
across the room in slow motion,
imagining the eye of a needle elastic enough
for entire graveyards, a tombstone at a time,
to pass through.

July 2008
Dallas

"Marshal Tojo, 1946"

He was an insignificant-looking little spectator
in the front row, just behind the seated war criminals
looking proud and inscrutable
like a row of carved idols.

Reaching across, too fast for the MPs to react,
he relieved himself of a sharp little slap,
an almost womanish, wasp-like rebuke,
striking the top of a gleaming, smooth-shaven head.

The dock was constructed of aromatic
cherrywood, smooth to the touch—
the army engineers, on this occasion,
did themselves proud.

Huge metal fan-blades
revolved slowly overhead,
unable to dispel the almost tropical
East Asian heat,

small beads forming magically like seed pearls
reappearing from under the handkerchief
almost as soon as it brushes the smooth
expanse of moist skin.

So many bald heads, rounded, glinting
in the hot merciless all-seeing light.

July 2008
Dallas

"Illumination #15"

A wasp dropped down from the ceiling,
stung the underside of my thumb
and flew off to die in the corner.

Oily-fingered greed
leaves traces and stains on the pages of a book
recording every lamentation under the sun.

Fighter pilots always seem to know what to do.
They sit around the mess, trading stories, inoculating
one another against the need to do something specific.

Demyan almost infected his fifth stenographer
with a dengue fever known as
individualised culpability.

Fear motivates with a searching pressurised plasticity
punching the wall in the diaphragm
between everyone else and the specialness
of what it feels like to wake up every morning
believing yourself to be separate.

August 2008
Dallas

A dying moth
dragged itself inside the jointed shell of
a huge, decaying hornet, the stings of which had
long ago rotted away—

a wannabe chisels his forgeries,
blundering in the mazes of heavyhanded
trial and error,
lusting for the veiled Muse to come
and dictate her divine inspiration,
nestling lines of thick-scripted intoxication
on the snowy white page.

Who can approximate the dictates of genius,
who inform the husked jointedness
of empty kernels and crushed seedpods of barley
like a daisy-chain twining its cluster of pomegranates
for some distracted captive to nibble?

Never has the sting of cold poison so numbingly
frozen and paralysed the lubricious oesophagus—

to be without inspiration,
wrestling with an angel's cold chastity
whispering to the coarsened husk of what's left:

impostor, parasite, stage-prop, window-dressing,
get ready to adorn a true Genius,
like the fly alighting on a cold marble brow.

August 2008
Dallas

"To Need Her (More Than Anything Else in the World)"

Last night I went to bed yearning for her caress,
the quicksand-like texture of her soft, cloying lips.

This morning I woke so drained
from the swirls and curlicues of my internal bloodletting,

I could scarcely drag myself down the stairs
and across the sagging, caved-in floorboards
of a house at war with itself.

I know I'm a fangful of poison,
    but would it be such ill grace for her to let slip
the dogs of her pretended compassion?

The jugular of my universe
    entwines itself
with her Jack-and-the-Beanstalk aorta,
throbbing ventricle with ventricle
to produce some sort of compromise,

but the streams and freshets run dry
as the amputated hand that once replenished them
continues somehow to keep manipulating
its nerveless, shellfish-like fingers.

I just can't seem to filter my emotions and feelings
  after opening vein after vein—

infusing them with enough red dye
to wash away all the traces of
infiltration and longing.

Love, lust, infatuation, desire—

words resemble fading drops of blood on a bandage,
taste like the bitter transparency
of a chemical refined and compounded
to the point of—
   unconsciousness.

September 2008
Dallas

"Song of the Garden"

Her unflappable coldness cracked
every bone in my body.

Her unassailable contempt ran me through like a sword.

The invisible wound
(like a teardrop of iridescent molybdenum)
couldn't make up its mind—

a smooth water-droplet on the outside
concealing powdery pain dry as dust on the inside,
tight-packed, like a blossom the size of a pinhead—

or long-lasting moisture imprisoned
(like the splash of colour vivifying a bruise)
within the swaying hump of a camel?

My flowerbed-vulnerability attracted hornets and wasps;
I remember the sweltering odour of jasmine
unsheathing itself just in time
for the wasps and hornets to sting one another,
a few even stinging themselves;

I watched the one whose bloodied sting
had embedded itself in the tip of my finger,
abdomen torn asunder,
just barely skimming the motionless tips of the spear-grass;

the ants would be picking her to pieces
before I could open the medicine cabinet and doctor myself.

A cool compress, numbing the sting,
making the swelling go down,

reminds me of the first girl whose
fragrant incense-like lips I ever imagined,
conjuring them night after night in my dreams—

Experience devours everything in its path,
buzzing like a swarm of hirsute bumblebees,
clearing away the dead flowers,
annihilating that which was merely taking up space.

September 2008
Dallas

"Cause and Effect"

Tenacity animated the swollen fingers,
her dying gasps like interminable bits of hot wax
burning the same spot on the back of your neck
again and again.

She raised my mother,
but only now have I entered the equation,
too late to be a variable at the equal-sign death-bed.

The stubbornness with which she clung to this ugly scene
of gasping and moaning, foul smells and spasms of pain,
somehow impressed itself in the soft clay of my mind.

My mother had severed the chain of cause and effect,
kept us apart for reasons best known to the two of them—

impatient for the old hag to die
so that I could get back to my keyboard
and continue plunking out the untuned chords
of a piece by Clementi,

I pursed my inexperienced lips,
trying to conceal my impatience.

At the last her eyes opened,
those clouded gas-jets of nothingness—
fastened like starved leeches
onto my suddenly tightly closed eyelids,

sucking the blood out of my eyes
as they rolled up in their sockets,
boring into the cotton-candy emptiness
within the dome of my skull.

A transfer had somehow achieved itself,
like a spark of dwindling electricity:

I gave her the sliced-off, gnawed tips of my selfishness,
my impatience for her to hurry up and get it over with—
and in return—

I dare not unravel the crepe-banded swaddling clothes—
of what her death impregnated me with—a little something,
small, wizened, wrinkled, newborn.

October 2008
Dallas

Like a hard little pea,
shriveled, pitted,
slipped under so many mattresses
the exacting sensibility cracks down the middle,

life teased me; I tried to give birth to myself
but somehow had a miscarriage—

I pickled my stillborn potential in a jar of formaldehyde,
the strangely expressive little purplish-red face
magnified and distorted through the curve of the glass.

Fascinated,
unable to turn away,
I tried unsuccessfully to suppress
the queer little twinge it gave me
in the pit of my stomach—

Like a hard little pellet,
shriveled, pitted, of opium,
dissolving almost as slowly
as our hopes and dreams for the future,
a single burning, smouldering
grain at a time.

October 2008
Dallas

"Birds of Prey #5"

Swathed in the folds of a crinkly chewing-gum wrapper,
my ruby-faceted heart was little more than a mouthful,
torn out from behind my piano-key ribs
like a palpitating, strangely shaped, dripping red gem.

Soaring on a turbulent updraft,
an ice-cold river of air many thousands of feet above
the furze-coloured countryside spread out
like a faded prayer shawl whose threads are unraveling,

the kestrel screams in a keen-edged ejaculation so shrill,
it freezes the blood, saps the instinct to hide oneself.

A goshawk devoured my heart.
A pilgrim falcon gobbled the soft layers of a brain
ever too feverish and fretful for its own good—

last of all, sparrows and chickadees pecked in my eyes,
drank the vitreous fluid, and left the white bone
of my denuded sockets to gleam in the morning sunlight.

October 2008
Dallas

The imitation cockatoo feathers
grafted onto the plucked nakedness
of a viciously predatory, sharp-taloned fledgling

wafted all sorts of bad dreams into my ridiculous little head
as I lay burning with fever—

I imagined a big fleshy lizard-like tail
waving and swaying behind me,
perfectly balanced so that I could run on two legs.

My fantasies were like some flawed yellow diamond
the size of a grain of sawdust
stuck to the sweaty thigh of an exhausted miner,
too small to be noticed, much less confiscated.

October 2008
Dallas

Billowing steam pushes
up out of the ground in clouds so thick and seething,
it condenses all over your face in scalding, steaming rivulets,
forces you backwards to a safe distance,

yearning, quivering
in the knife-like cold
that seeps into the marrow of your exhausted,
fever-filled bones.

You caress, prick, spur and then curse yourself,
poised quivering between perfectly balanced,
mutually repulsive
temptations.

November 2008
Dallas

My curiosity forded a stream.

The flat bannock-shaped stones
shimmering a light blue
in the glassy chattering water

had become so rounded and slippery,
they tilted underfoot, sliding and shifting,
exposing sharp little rocks which like serrated teeth

bit into the foot-like sensitivity of my
exquisite need (shaped and angled by the flow of time)
to know what had happened.

Losing its balance, my curiosity
up-ended itself and fell sideways,
carried downstream by the violence of an

unexpected thaw with all its tons of
melting snow trickling and coming together,
swelling into an irresistible flood.

The subconscious washes away everything in its path,
carving fresh channels
in the soft clay of forgetfulness.

November 2008
Dallas

"The Shape of Things to Come"

The rapaciousness of the sharp-talon'd fledgling
cheeping and screaming for its
bits of raw flesh torn out of a carcase
in which (as often as not) the heart
still senselessly spasms and fibrillates—

tearing them from its parent's upraised beak,
insatiable, bruising its downy, oversized-looking head
on the rocks below as it stretches a scrawny,
    vulture-like neck
to slurp up the streaks and spatters of warm salty blood—

The shape of things to come
like swirling smoke under glass
lurks in reptilian, cold-blooded eyes
first hatched how many thousands of
generations ago?

Once I had a dream about a fledgling
that looked just like all the others,
but hesitated, smelling the
warm blood for the first time,

and all the universe strained, panting,
tongue hanging out,

and I waited to see whether
it dripped blood,
or saliva.

November 2008
Dallas

"End of the World #16"

A smell of burning filled the air,
asphyxiating cinders mixed with papery ash.

Everything in the distance was grey;
the edge of sight was beginning to rise up—

a wall of something dark and wet
scraping the clouds.

The ground was starting to buckle and split
as the roaring of the wave pounded
our brains and spinal cords to jelly,

flung us into the mixing bowl, and
kneaded our consciousness—

It must've been spawned in the guts of a nightmare—
a seismic disturbance cracking the planet in two,
displacing all the billions of tons
of thundering, piling-up ocean—

five thousand feet high, engulfing the clouds—

I sit hunched, blaspheming my fate,
heart hammering, forehead plastered,
the damp ringlets of hair sopping wet—

Waiting in slow motion for the inconceivable impact,
preparing myself for the shock of—infinity.

December 2008
Dallas

At the end of its strength,
like a fly trapped in an upside down bowl,
the world I lived in opened its veins.

Existence heaved a gut-wrenching sigh that
reverberated to the back of beyond,
a cataclysm mistaken by some for the nightmare yell
of bucking-bronco apocalypse breaking
the framework of its constraining cradle to bits.

I try to bite off my hand at the wrist,
but find my teeth to be too worn down,
blunted, susceptible to the pain of meeting
the slightest resistance,
jaws clenched, till the pressure surpasses endurance.

The world I wanted to live in
decamped years ago,
leaving the sort of world that doesn't have the vision
to put its head in a noose and kick the chair out from under its
wildly swinging,
  by degrees relaxing,
    slackening, feet—

but instead steeps itself in a bath of warm water,
laving its hurts and lacerations,
numbing itself as the water slowly turns
from pink to dark red—

The world is sick;
it was sick from cradle to grave,
and I only hope as we perform the Last Rites,
that it precedes me, lighting the way down
a twisting turning path full of sharp stones.

December 2008
Dallas

"On a Night Like This"

Stinging kernels of sleet and sharpened fragments of ice
scour my face as the screaming wind
flings them in gusty fistfuls
making me long for the warmth of the fire-pit
with its hissing embers, drowsy flickering shadows,
and blissfully seductive sensations of
compromise and surrender.

A crust of ice crunches underfoot
(crunches like teeth biting into an apple)
as I lead myself by an invisible ring in the nose
down a treacherous path,
walking slowly and carefully.

Encrustations of hoarfrost and rime begin
thickening along the eaves of the chapel glazed with
hanging fingers of ice
that clink and snap off in the wind.

Only on a cold night like this
do my stale orisons (for the eternal repose of the dead)
seem to rise, like warm air, mounting higher and higher,
at last deflected off the coldness of the star-studded
firmament, shooting back, like a boomerang,
to pierce a heart full of warm, smoking blood.

January 2009
Dallas

We surged and, jostling one another,
passed back and forth the splintery box

as rifles discharged deafeningly
straight up at the sky as if to bring down
the sun and the moon, the clouds and the wind.

Chanting in unison we scourge ourselves,
breathe burning ashes, fall on knives,
set arms and legs on fire, ecstatic,

eyes filming over, screaming, twisting,
unable somehow to face the fact
that death has come like a thief in the night:

the old breaks down,
the new condemns itself,
and nothing lasts forever.

Who once served pearls, now pearly love
dispenses with upside-down contempt.

January 2009
Dallas

138

The squibs and rockets gave off
a fading comet-like trail of ruby red
peppered with curlicues of blinding white light
which forced the goshawks flitting overhead
to avert their rapacious, overbright eyes.

Never has my pain felt so strangely remote;
never has my loneliness gasped for breath
quite so studiedly.

A corpse-like mutedness,
fiercely ineffectual in everything
but its raging infectiousness,
makes me feel like a corner of myself,

a dividing line,

the beginning of some things,
the shunting-off of secretly cherished ideals
suffocated for want of the denigration
resulting from contact—
an opening up, a broadening, a diffusion of heat.

It feels like the end of a life.
The monumentality of a single corner
on the edge of a lopsided crevice—
dwarfs everything else.

January 2009
Dallas

An ocean once doffed its plumed hat to a raindrop
shivering all alone in the cold.

In between, a puddle reflects
the jackdaws nesting overhead—
but not their echoing chatter, nor the
smell of their eggs.

Every raindrop strains against its own globular perfection
the way light taps at that same roundness,
enticed by its crystal-ball subtlety.

What must it feel like as the
liquid making up your particular substance and shape
voids itself, merging with the boundless,
the collective, the safety and warmth of being
deaf, dumb, and blind?

A hanging droplet can only refract the sunlight,
bending the shackled brightness to the critical degree
just short of breakage—
to free the thronging, throbbing colours of the
heterodox, heretical rainbow.

January 2009
Dallas

Shreds of cartilage with bits of sinewy gristle
line the gut of the pregnant peregrine dipping her beak
in the stream to wash off the traces of blood.

Masses of fragmented, faceted schist
glister and sparkle, pushed up through the crust
to the pitted, flaking surface crisscrossed with wrinkles,

a cemetery of tormented rills leading nowhere,
a festival to the almighty Dead End.

Still the birds of prey go on gorging themselves,
jettisoning rat skulls which crumble to powder
in the shifting layers of leaf-mould
accumulating over the squelching bog
with its secrets, its mummification,
its deep-delving fingers seeking to jab the earth's core.

A dimly remembered atavistic anguish creeps forth
amidst the downy carpet of feathers
surrounding the bits of eggshell
surrounding the cracked ribs and thighbones
surrounding the nest
made of just about everything under the sun.

Convolvulus blossoms decompose in the fever
rippling invisibly in dancing heatwaves
filling the forest and spilling to the salt-tang'd astringency
of the cleansing, medicinal, spume-crested breakers.

A keen shrilling on the buffeting wind
draws the glance upward to embrace
the wheeling sweep of seabirds.

It seems the sharp-beaked predators that nest in the treetops
have followed us—the gulls have dispersed.

Winking tetrahedron crystals of rosaceous quartz
going off in firecracker flashes wherever the sunbeams
poke and jab their way through the clouds
remind us of growth, decay, and rebirth.

Cathedrals obliterate all trace
of the original embryonic wigwam.

Shaggy-tufted brows jutting out
protect the eyes for a reason.

The legato carriage and gait of the slow-stepping housecat
suggest the rollicking canter of the lean, sculpted sabre-tooth
springing for the throat that resonates
with the birth of these words.

January 2009
Dallas

His head was shaped like an indestructible box
filled with crumbling fragments of something that was both
sweet-smelling and poisonous.

His so-called character pirouetted and bobbed to the surface
in the arresting shape of his grotesquely fascinating skull.

A lying con-artist,
he brought his misbegotten gifts to bear
in the heads of gullible young girls whose breath,
warm and fragrant with youth, could have
floated a ship of the line.

I followed him.
I ran him through.
I killed him.

Revenge has been called the sweetest thing on earth.
For me it left a bitter taste in the mouth—
a sudden knowledge of all the pathways closed off
irrevocably, punched shut with an invisible padlock.

His skull was like a series of coffins fitting inside one another—
always another enclosed sarcophagus to try and force open.

January 2009
Dallas

You need to turn and face the churning,
mile-high tornado of your burning visceral fear
as it tears up the field,
bearing down on the flimsy ramshackle house
thrown together without even the refuge
of a rickety closet.

Seeding the scarred, pitted
surface of the planet was always
thirsty work, or so the alcoholic with
bloodshot eyes and stinking breath intimates.

Gathering in the harvest with its weeds and blistering nettles,
masses of bitter-smelling wisteria,
your back begins aching,
drops of sweat collecting just above your eyebrows,
stinging moisture flicking from the ends of your lashes
each time you unconsciously blink.

February 2009
Dallas

Vast somethings collide in the mist,
causing milkmaids to slip
on the wet grass
and go flying.

Every full-throated scream
bouncing off the roof
of its own mouth
ultimately gathers
a bucket of scorpions
in the thick red sludge of the river delta,

rainbow-coloured irrigation channels
doubling back on themselves,

the four corners of the reason why
methodically rounded
the way housewives
brown a steak in the frying-pan—

the way a snake eating its own tail
can be picked up and
rolled off the side of a cliff.

February 2009
Dallas

"Slivers of Seeing"

Cut off the head of a cockroach,
and it can sometimes still breathe, keeping itself
darkly, tenaciously, strangely alive.

Does hard living blear the flatness of used-up-looking
eyes which haven't twinkled or flashed sparks of anger
in g-d knows how long?

The day was already terrifically, irreversibly
sprocketed, like a sliver of celluloid
gathering dust on the cutting room floor.

Can you feel the sunset punching itself
into a million flashing, jagged-edged slivers?

Tremulous parents crane their necks, anxiously scanning
the periphery for the first sign of children
grown sure of themselves, uncompromising,
full of moral righteousness,

but most frightening of all:
totally free of even the most half-hearted,
residual squeamishness.

February 2009
Dallas

Attempt a middle course, and the durable wax
holding our feathers in place
begins to soften, the giddy liquefaction
of steaming globs tearing loose and dropping
from all along the disintegrating
uselessness of what a moment ago
kept us soaring—

it reminds us of the terrible price to be paid
when freefall usurps
the functionality
of lips and tongue and glib teeth
about to be pulverised
on the jaggedly granite coastline
rushing fist first to meet us.

February 2009
Dallas

Instead of cursing and gnashing my teeth,
I deface what crosses my path, idealise what doesn't
the way a meandering drop of blood
leaves a red zigzag.

My conscience pieced together the shards of a nightmare:
all of us were defenceless and vulnerable.

Varyags know the battle rhythm,
ceaselessly praising past feats of revenge,

ululating past efforts at having stayed afloat
for almost as long as seventeen and three-sixteenths of a second,

creating future pride
like a rock, a foundation of stone—

like the fading stains
running up and down the beams of a scaffold—

Chaos pours down with a mechanistic brutality,
sadistically teaching a handful of us,
every few hundred years or so,
to be merciful.

February 2009
Dallas

"Hot Date"

It felt ghastly—
my mind's trash in its quivering shapelessness—
the accumulated residual refuse
of sticky-slippery solicitations,
manipulation, betrayal—

the palsied snapping and grabbing
of a maladaptive sledgehammer-like pincer—

all this—ugliness—was turned over and over,
tumbling, shuffling, intermixing

like a lottery whose 'prize'
is abjudged to be the emotion
best attuned to whatever hand touches it.

I lay perspiring her thick, rich sweat,
watching her cry my little tears.

February 2009
Dallas

149

"Unanswerable"

Fear tastes acrid.
Your tongue swells,
the pimply taste-buds hardening,
drying out from the inside.

Many years ago
I served in the Presidential palace.

Our President was unforgiving,
irascible, pigheaded—
but he also possessed moral strength;
he was a strong, courageous—
but fallible—man.

Last night the police turned up at my door,
'invited' me to go with them—

whizzing through the outskirts of the sleeping city,
turning onto the highway,
a hot dry wind lifting our hair
with practiced, invisible fingers,

they explained that I was wanted
for purposes of identification.

My mind raced. As a functionary
serving our late President and his family,
I had seen him many times, but was far removed
from the levers and pulleys of destiny.

Surely others, more intimate, less
'in the dark' so to speak, could have been rounded up?

Unless, indeed, I was the only one left.

ii.

Some things embedded in the mould of the past
are poisonous to touch or inhale,
even to brush the wingtips
of flitting memory against in passing—
we don't go back, for some things.

I remember the blood.

Blood staining the skulking assassins
disguised as army officers,
staining epaulettes and sleeves, dripping
from tassels, staining and splotching
the plush velvet of state rooms—
dripping from curtains—
dripping everywhere, in pools
on the marble stair-steps,
the stench of coagulating blood rising
from the sewers tricking and gurgling—

how much blood does it take to make
the drains scream with a gurgling sound?

I didn't see any killing, nor even hear any gunshots.
But I saw the blood, even after averting my eyes.
I inhaled the sickly stench after stuffing my nostrils.

iii.

Our convoy (composed of government officials,
soldiers, the informant leading them to the
unmarked mass grave, and of course vans and jeeps

151

stuffed with labourers—to do the actual digging)
turned off the highway after a brief consultation
and began to snake its way much more slowly
across the wasteland of undulating acclivities,
intersecting gullies, small flat-topped hills
indistinct under the thick clouds
blindfolding heaven's
vigilant stars—

why is it that graves of this particular sort,
unmarked, meant to lie undiscovered,
should exude such a palpable, constricting,
heart-crushing loneliness?

Any grave would be sad enough,
but this square mile or so rested like something
heavy and suffocating, strangling
the nation's breath, squeezing off the
windpipe of its raspy-throated,
stentorian future.

After several more lengthy pauses,
dark shapes pointing, gesticulating,
their argumentative, frantic whispering
carried like a dead thing on the
eddying undulations of the
lukewarm breeze in its decaying,
slow-motion death throes,

we seemed to be going in circles,
and I was beginning to doze off when with a
sharper than usual jolt of the brakes we
screeched to a halt, everyone climbing forth
to stretch tired limbs and, clumping together
in groups (according to one's station),
await the inevitable.

iv.

More pointing and whispering. At last
the orders were given, and the digging
commenced. I gazed spellbound at
sandy crumbling clods which flew from rusted
shovels, dry dust seeping into the nostrils.

The digging started and stopped several times.
Towards dawn I was roughly shaken
from torpid sleep, and, disoriented,
trembling against the desert chill,
was led over towards a vast ochre mound
of displaced, disemboweled-looking earth.

I was barely able to stand. Two soldiers had to
support me. For the first time I understood
the awful thing they had brought me to do.

Shreds of tattered cloth, strips of tarpaulin
were being prised from clumps of mud
mixed with sand—
a soft giving way of rotted substances
too eaten away by the elements
to tear, much less break, assaulted the eardrum
with an attenuated tenacity.

v.

Soldiers had to keep nudging, prodding me—
I unwillingly turned my shrinking gaze back
to the nuts and bolts of this macabre excavation.
The first bone—possibly a humerus—followed by the
two pieces of a shattered thigh
brought the gorge rising in my throat.

The first skull with its contemplative sockets
watched me doubling over, trying again and again
to purge myself of what I was seeing.

I was ordered in guttural tones to make the
identification. It was like talking to
deaf signposts—I tried to make them
understand that a pile of bones, disembodied
skulls covered with encrustations of sand, hanging
strips of mud hinting at the tenacity of leftover
tresses embedded in filth—I explained as
coherently as I could that bones, skulls,
the stench of death—this undeniably
constituted a mass grave,
but as to the bodies interred—they could be
tribesmen, wandering Kurds, nomadic
shepherds killed in the crossfire of some
meaningless skirmish.

My exhausted captors irritably, menacingly, shoved
notarised paperwork for me to validate
with a quick signature.

vi.

Even as I shook my head, and their sullen
impatience threatened to explode—
my imprisoned glance
happened to take in some sort of
mud-crusted footwear—
an orthopaedic, prosthetic boot—

And I knew.

The President's sister was lame.
She had walked almost as naturally

as any other woman, with the aid not of
any other such boot on earth—but only
this one—I don't know how I recognised it
with such certainty, nor how I kept myself together
for the remaining time it took me to sign
their documentation and sit hunched,
eyes closed, as I was driven back
in the early morning, sternly admonished
to keep silent, on pain of death—

I remembered so vividly.

Like a dam breaking,
the images, emotions, tears
overwhelmed me as I curled up
on my bedroom floor
and howled like an animal.

Again and again I saw the sad-faced lady,
a streak of grey in her hair,
limping through the opulence of
Presidential palaces, seated at State dinners,
always two, or at most, three persons down
from her brother, the President.

I saw his piercing brown eyes, the thick
eyebrows growing into each other, knitting
with a spasm of unreasonable anger,

or just as often crowsfeet of laughter
wrinkling the corners of his burning eyes,
making accomplices of every onlooker—
the grandchildren, giggling, smiling,
all of whom were killed along with
the rest of their family—even down to
the newborn.

vii.

As I near the end of my undistinguished,
unremarkable life, I ask myself
what are we?

It seems to be so easy
to look down at a squalling infant,
flip an internal switch,
and pull the trigger.

The 'switch' is worse than the trigger—
the switch *invented* the trigger.

Again I ask myself: what *are* we?
In the name of Allah the Compassionate:
what have we become?

March 2009
Dallas

"White Girl"

Like a fine-grained, clinging residue
she fills the empty space of my hourglass mind,

my consciousness itching
to reflect itself all the way to infinity
as if confronting two panes of silvered glass
face to face, almost touching.

She amazes, baffles,
puts things together like two card-decks
shuffled and scrunched into a single rickety holder.

She spills each of my ten thousand
thimble-shaped eyes
with her two indescribable
treasures of seeing—

If I could describe them—
  if I could sneak up in the dark…

March 2009
Dallas

In the imagination of what slouching, rough beast
was I first conceived, squeezed through the wringer,
shaped and glibly perverted?

She who bore me was killed roller-skating;
her skull smacked into a low-hanging tree branch.

The Wet Nurse ran off with a scullery maid
she was said to have nicknamed 'Cinderella'
(and later abandoned in turn).

My foster parents were too busy gambling
on futures and junk bonds and toxic debt packages
to pay me much mind.

Perhaps if left to my own tired devices,
like a spindly weed unable to get enough sunlight—

I might have actually wormed my way through
some narrow, unguarded breach
in my developing character.

The living tomb inhabited by a blind-deaf-mute
strikes me as almost tangentially enviable—

At least the numbing deprivation
accords a sort of stuntedly shrinkwrapped,
stultifying, but ironclad, protection.

March 2009
Dallas

He used lots of big words
to gum up the intricate functioning
of my stopwatch-like mind,

defining *x* as *y*,
yx as *xyz* squared—
teaching that werewolves
can order the world to their liking.

Now I stagnate behind a pair of dark glasses;
the windows of my soul have been daubed
with black paint.

March 2009
Dallas

A particle of chafing, burning slumber
lit up the mind engrossed with wakefulness.

There's more than meets the eye.

There's less than bleeds the heart.

In between,
the minefields crammed with ticking nightmares
would task the most talented seamstress

pulling out little squidges of silk
in the slits crawling like millions of ants
up and down the puffed sleeves

rising like a bubble of blood
bursts above the blow-hole

of an intractable tumour
lanced just a few seconds
too late.

March 2009
Dallas

160

She promised to explicate
the red pain, the green pain, the black pain—
to break it all down.

I didn't exactly believe she could do this,
didn't think her steady-handed enough
to dissect the bleeding colours of a rainbow in torment.

Maybe she was so bewilderingly enigmatic and yet
at the same time irresistible
because she pulled the wool so skillfully
down over my squinting eyelids

ready to blink
at the slightest twinge
of the invisible tripwire strung

from inside my left tearduct
across the finely moulded bridge of my nose
to the other equally lachrymose gland.

I wept as she promised me the sun and the moon.

Tears slid down the ski slope of my
angular cheekbone as she regarded me
with unblinking, unflinching detachment.

March 2009
Dallas

For the simple reason that words constitute quicksand,
and despite the fact that Silence, golden or no,
can become a thousand times more clinging
than the seething mist of hot rage—

I recommend a navigational override;
sew your lips together
with a spool of black thread.

February 2009
Dallas